STILL
STANDING

STILL STANDING

A Lent course based on the Elton John movie ROCKETMAN

RACHEL MANN

DARTON · LONGMAN + TODD

First published in 2020 by
Darton, Longman and Todd Ltd
1 Spencer Court
140–142 Wandsworth High Street
London SW18 4JJ

Print book ISBN: 978-0-232-53491-7
eBook ISBN: 978-0-232-53492-4

A catalogue record for this book is available from the British Library.

Camera logo by Senhikari Studio/shutterstock.com
Designed and produced by Judy Linard
Printed and bound in Great Britain by Bell & Bain, Glasgow

CONTENTS

INTRODUCTION

In Matthew's gospel, Jesus famously says, 'Unless you change and become like little children, you will never enter the Kingdom of Heaven.' For those of us – who through temperament, or job role, or because of the responsibility which has come to us – live very 'grown-up' lives, Jesus' statement is especially challenging. Indeed, there have been times when if I'd had the chance, I would have liked to take Jesus aside and ask him what on earth he is on about. While the recent coronavirus pandemic and the pressures generated by the ongoing climate crisis may have challenged many of us about our priorities, it is still the case that, for many of us, we are not going to escape our adult responsibilities and demands any time soon. Much as some of us might hope to 'rescope' our lives, the need to earn a living, or the demands of parenthood and so on, is not going to disappear. Jesus might expect us to become little children if we are to enter the Kingdom of Heaven, but it can seem an impossible request to fulfil.

Rocketman, the biopic about rock superstar Elton John, might strike some as, at best, a surprising and, at worst, an outrageous choice as the basis for a Lent course. There are no two ways about it, Sir Elton Hercules John has lived a life of excess and naughtiness that few, even in the world of rock and roll music, can match. It is worth saying, at the outset, that the film on which this course is based is 15 rated, and contains language of the strongest, earthiest sort, and depicts scenes which some will find challenging. So why select this film for a Lent course, if it is likely to upset many people? Well, perhaps, because underneath the drug-taking, the bad language and the random sexual encounters, *Rocketman* arguably presents the story of a person seeking not only redemption, but what it means to become a little child.

In *Rocketman*, we witness Elton's forty-year journey to becoming reconciled with the little child he effectively left behind when he, as one character puts it, moved on from 'the person he was born to be'. Elton was christened Reginald Kenneth Dwight, an only child from suburban Pinner, who grew up to become a talented pianist. That talented pianist discovered a gift for song writing and performance and, in due course, became the world-wide sensation that is 'Elton Hercules John'. What followed is legend: decades of excess, tantrums, diva-like behaviour and wild living.

Some Christians, with very good reason, will argue that Elton's behaviour during his 1970s and 1980s pomp was far from mature. It was the behaviour of a 'man-child'. Certainly when Jesus invites us to become like 'little children', it is hardly on the atavistic model shown by Elton at his most excessive and bleak. Nonetheless, it is a story to conjure with. *Rocketman* provides an extraordinary leaping-off point to explore what redemption, friendship, love, identity and hope mean in a compromised and compromising world. Elton's story – which shows him both acting up and acting out in order to cope with a prejudiced and unloving world, as well as ultimately finding peace – is a story with which many of us can identify.

Of course, at the heart of *Rocketman* is one of the greatest soundtracks in popular music history. Tracks like 'Song for Guy', 'Tiny Dancer', and the title song are part of the substrate of western popular culture. For me, one of the bravest and most brilliant gambits in this movie is its decision to be what is known as a 'jukebox musical'. That is, it uses Elton's music as a way of telling his autobiography and constructing the story. These songs – written with his long-term writing partner Bernie Taupin – count among the classics of popular music. One of the striking characteristics of the film is that in using these songs to structure Elton's story, it does so through lyrics written primarily by Bernie. In some ways, this is Bernie's story too, or at least a story about how he sees and relates to his old friend through their songs. Whatever else one might feel about the appropriateness of *Rocketman* as the basis for a serious Lenten study, it provides one of the finest pop music soundtracks available. Elton's capacity to bring joy and pleasure to millions through his music is beyond question. I hope that even those who quail at using *Rocketman* as the basis for a Lent study will enjoy a good singalong.

Nonetheless, I do understand why some may be sceptical about *Rocketman's* capacity to hold Lenten themes. The first forty years of Elton's life – which provides the setting for this film – arguably represents the precise opposite of what we might anticipate during Lent. *Rocketman* shows us a life shaped by wild living and excess, whereas Lent, for most people, is either about giving things up or finding a way to go deeper with God. This work of going deeper is typically predicated on developing one's Christian discipline (either in prayer or in action). Lent typically takes us out into the wilderness with Jesus. In the wilderness he does not eat or drink for forty days and he resists the temptations of the devil. By contrast, as Elton acknowledges during therapy near the start of the film, he has essentially never resisted a thing. In his story, temptation is repeatedly embraced, and often with sheer abandon.

However, I am convinced that Elton's story enables the attentive viewer to explore other kinds of wilderness. I am not for a second suggesting he is some sort of modern-day Jesus. Rather, his addictions and identity struggles indicate extreme versions of the kind of wilderness experiences many of us face in the privileged countries of the Economic North. Arguably, these are wildernesses of the mind and soul which are predicated on excess and access to abundant distraction. Some believe that, in the shadow of COVID-19 and other emergent crises (around, for example, the climate), humanity will learn new ways of living and lessons about how to flourish. That is yet to be seen. In the meantime, part of *Rocketman*'s power lies not so much in the way it shows us how to live in a Christ-like way, as in what it can mean to come through temptation, excess and the wilderness of modern life. In doing so we may become more fully like Jesus and thereby more fully ourselves. The stories of Christ and Elton are, unsurprisingly, quite distinct. That doesn't mean the specifics of Elton's story don't provide leaping-off points for our own journeys of faith, hope and love.

I think it is worth acknowledging my own interest in *Rocketman*. While I think it is worthy of Lenten study in its own right, I feel I have a personal stake in the story. Before I unpack that, it's worth saying that when I was young, back in the 1980s, I didn't have much time for Elton John. He struck me as a washed-up, overblown showman who was beloved of middle-brow, middle-aged suburbanites, scared of real music. Teenagers really are so judgmental, aren't they? I wanted either authentic, gritty folk, complex progressive music or brain-shattering metal. I wanted something to shout about.

By the time I was really aware of Elton's output, he was in a real mess and his music had lost focus. It was only in my twenties that, as someone who was serious about music and had survived my own 'rock and roll' crises, I began to realise that Elton and his song writing partner Bernie Taupin were bona fide geniuses. Looking back it comes as no surprise that Elton came more clearly into focus in my life as I came to terms with my own identity and sexuality struggles.

I have, then, a degree of identification with Elton. While I would never even begin to claim the level of musical talent he has, music became one of my outlets for survival. As a teenager I'd picked up a guitar, first in an attempt to look cool, and then as a means of coping with the world. It gave me something to 'go to' when I was stressed, lost or bewildered. I'd practise for hour upon hour each day and was sufficiently competent by my early twenties to consider, briefly, a career as a rock musician. More significantly, I was caught-up in the rock and roll lifestyle. Between the age of 18 and 23 I took a huge amount of drugs. From the age of 16 until I was 23 I was a serious drinker. Part of the attraction of drugs – which many are not prepared to admit – is that they can be fun. If, like me, one is a 'performing introvert' – i.e. someone who likes to be centre-stage but actually finds it distressing – then drugs and alcohol can offer ways of fabricating confidence.[1]

The power of mind-altering substances to fabricate a semblance of confidence is absolutely one of the themes of *Rocketman*. Ultimately, the film reveals the emptiness of drug use. Equally, Elton has to negotiate a world in which his sexuality is under constant question. Indeed, pre-1967, homosexuality in the UK was criminalised and it was only decades later that it was properly decriminalised. Both growing up and as a young man, Elton lived in a society where being gay was treated with fear and disgust rather than respect. Elton, like a lot of gay men of that era, had to come to terms with who he was in ways which can seem surprising in more enlightened times. Arguably, drugs and alcohol became props and crutches to cope. My story, while

---

[1] In the closing stages of the film, Elton's step-dad calls him a 'performing introvert'.

different, has that dimension too. As a trans woman I had to come to terms with myself. When I struggled with self-acceptance, drugs gave me a way of blotting out, temporarily, who I was.

I cannot be alone in finding in *Rocketman* powerful personal connections. However, I don't think you have to have struggled with identity and confidence to see universal themes in the film. It has the power to speak into the wider ups-and-downs and twists and turns of any life. I have long been convinced that the Christian life is a call to life in all its fullness. What is also clear to me is that this is a life which is not readily achieved. Things like drugs and drink and seeking after highs in all their varieties can masquerade as short-cuts to the fullness of life – believe me, I've tried most of them! – but they have an emptiness built into them. To grow in Christ's likeness is a lifetime's work, often with many false starts and twists and turns. This is demonstrated in technicolour in Elton John's case. All of us, however, live versions of the half-healed and half-lived life.

As the great spiritual writer Thomas Merton reminds us in *The Seeds of Contemplation,* it is very difficult for human beings, living with the gift of free will and the costs of sin, to offer glory to God in an unsullied way. We struggle to be our true selves. He contrasts how difficult humans find it to offer glory to God with how easy it is for a tree to show glory. He suggests that a tree does not struggle to offer glory because it cannot choose to be other than a tree. An oak tree shows forth praise for God by growing tall and wide and growing leaves and producing acorns, etc. However, because humans have free-will we can turn away from giving glory and growing into the likeness of Christ. We can be other than we are called to be. Indeed, because of our deep woundedness, and because of structural and personal sin, it becomes a lifetime's work to become ever more Christlike.

It is sometimes claimed that one of the curious

effects of modern life is that no one ever truly grows up. This theme of extended adolescence and inability to take responsibility is reflected in so-called 'culture war' debates on the supposed difference between 'millennials' – often stereotyped as flaky, over-indulged and sensitive – and 'boomers' – presented as selfish, self-centred, greedy and boorish. Equally, the newish word 'adulting' has been coined to indicate when younger adults feel they have stepped into unwelcome adult responsibilities or have crossed the threshold of responsibilities traditionally reserved for adults. In his recent hugely popular book, *Humankind*, historian Rutger Bregman suggests that the evolutionary success of humans is predicated on a kind of positive, social immaturity. He calls humanity 'homo puppy' to indicate that we are, by nature, socially playful, sociable and in need of strokes.

Rocketman is, arguably, a study in two almost contradictory things: firstly, how a person who never properly grows up learns to be an adult. Elton, via a life of wealth, drug-induced excess, and irresponsibility, falls into near despair and finally learns to take responsibility. However, running alongside that is another direction of travel. For *Rocketman* is also a study in how an adult – who has all the power, cynicism and mistrust that can go with that status – learns how to be a child again. One of the ways in which *Rocketman* is redemptive is by showing that even the most cynical and damaged person can learn to trust, love and begin again. An adult can become as open, playful and hopeful as a child.

I have long believed that you cannot keep a good God down. You cannot, to use a word we've learned to use since the COVID-19 pandemic, keep God in 'lockdown'. We might try to lock him up or kill him, but he rises again to greet us with love, hope and the promise of reconciliation. God is always waiting to meet us, and sometimes this place of encounter lies in the oddest of places. We rightly might expect to meet God in a work of art, or the wonders of nature, perhaps even in a great piece of music. We expect to meet him in the breaking of bread and wine outpoured. Why not in a popular film too?

I know *Rocketman* won't be for everyone. Some will find it too outrageous. However, I also believe that if one dares to take a proper, closer look and place it in the context of the greatest story of all, one might be in for a surprise. Elton is no Jesus figure, nor is he an angel. However, he is a fascinating and extraordinary human being who has much to teach us about what it is to journey authentically in search of love, friendship, hope and grace.

HOW TO USE THIS BOOK

As with my previous DLT Lent book, *From Now On*, based on *The Greatest Showman*, I am disinclined to be overly prescriptive. While this is a Lent course designed to have both enough 'give' and enough direction to provide a group with sufficient material to chew on over five sessions, this is also a course that can be used profitably by a person reflecting and praying on their own.

Crucially, I have aimed to provide sufficient material that a course leader, or leaders, feel confident to plot their own path through each session. I want there to be an abundance of material to provide stimulation for a group or individual's journey through Lent. I'm sure that some groups, over a period of two hours, say, might gad their way through every section of a session. At the same time, not every group will be able to set aside more than half-an-hour or an hour. I commend, in such circumstances, a permissive approach. Never feel you have to slavishly work your way through every detail, question or even biblical section contained in the course. Please do add alternative biblical passages if you find examples that work better than mine.

It is also worth noting that, in the light of COVID-19 and what lockdown revealed about the power of digital ways of gathering, groups should not feel they have to meet physically in order to study together. There are a lot of online applications out there that can bring people together. Even I, who am frankly something of an analogue person in a digital age, have found value in using different applications to connect with others. It does not, for example, take an enormous amount of skill or perseverance to learn how to share a screen with other participants in, say, a Zoom meeting. This should mean that it is possible for someone with a digital version of the film to share a clip with others in an online group.

It should go without saying that, for participants to get the best out of this study guide, it is really helpful for them to have watched the film. For those who wish to study *Rocketman* in a group setting, it can be especially helpful for participants to watch the film together. For those of us of a musical turn, it can actually be fun to turn that 'watch-party' into a singalong. It is also worth saying that if the course is being followed in a socially-distant manner, and the film is available on a digital platform like Netflix, there are browser apps available to enable people to watch together, simultaneously, and be able to make real time comments. Please note that the timings in the course are based on the DVD sections. Do double check the timings if you are using Blu-ray or digital formats.

I trust that anyone who decides to follow this course will be alert to the fact that it is a 15 rated movie. I am conscious that some Christians have concerns about films that contain – as *Rocketman* does – lots of swearing, scenes of drunkenness and drug-taking, as well as sex. It perhaps says more about me than anything else, that as someone who – as a young person – had a taste for the rock and roll lifestyle and both enjoyed it and was messed up by it, that I don't think this film takes Elton's excesses lightly. It is hardly a morality tale, and if it were, I don't think it would be half so entertaining or ultimately affective and powerful. However, ultimately, I think it places Elton's struggles with his sexuality, his need for love and his personal insecurities in the proper perspective: he comes to a place of self-acceptance and joy, where his commitment to his future husband, David Furnish, should be celebrated. It is a hopeful story which handles the realities of Elton's life with authenticity.

However, I am conscious that not every Christian reads the world through the prism I bring to bear. Depending on your context, it may be worth warning more conservative members of a study group that this is a movie which has grown-up themes. However, I don't think you should labour this. It is a film badged as okay for anyone over the age of fifteen. There are some reasonably inventive uses of English in *Rocketman,* but the swearing is not much worse than what might be found in, say, *The King's Speech*.

For those leading and using this study guide I think there is another factor to take into account: the effect *Rocketman* might have on people who have faced prejudice about their sexuality or those who have survived drug and alcohol abuse. *Rocketman* has the power to speak into some of the more challenging and concealed aspects of our lives. I've been a priest long enough not easily to be shocked by either the heights or depths of the human condition. In the midst of my ministry I've been moved by some remarkable personal disclosures, often from people who appear to have their lives 'together'. Sometimes, those very people have been carrying sites of shame and pain in their heads and bodies for decades, without another human being beginning to realise.

Rocketman explores themes of identity, sexuality, alcohol, sex and drug addiction which are more ubiquitous than most people realise. It would be crass for those leading this Lent course to assume that everyone in a group has lived a life without struggle, abuse or personal complexity. More of us have negotiated personal and family mess than some churches are prepared to credit. It can be tempting for Christians to act as if everyone in a church has a neat, ordered and vanilla middle-class life. Few of us do, behind the public façade.

I guess I am saying that should someone disclose something personally vulnerable, it is crucial for group leaders and the wider group to hold those disclosures appropriately. It is worth stating from the outset that a high level of confidentiality will be expected within the group setting, as well as the best safeguarding standards within the Church. Leaders may wish to have to hand access to helplines for anyone struggling with addiction or working out their sexuality. We owe it to each other to look out for and look after each other.

The best way for us to do this is through prayer. Prayer is not simply saying words or keeping silence. It is an intentional relationship between God, us and each other. It is a way of being in the world. This course is structured through prayer. I offer an opening and closing prayer, but course leaders are welcome to add in other prayer elements as they see fit. Even if you find my prayers unhelpful, I hope no one skips over a short time of prayer at the beginning and end of the session. Some leaders may wish to provide a formal liturgy or quiet time. Group members might wish to lead worship in turn. Those who wish to work with this course individually may wish to weave it into their personal prayer and tradition.

One further note: I am conscious that using a movie for

study purposes can exclude those with visual impairment. Every adaptation to include participants should be considered. In parish, we always use subtitles when we show a film and where possible, add in audio description.

Ultimately, however, I do hope that this course is both stimulating and fun. I'm not one of those Christians who think that Lent requires a complete suspension of joy. *Rocketman* is not a po-faced film and I hope that as you work through the material in *Still Standing* that, in the midst of the deeper journey, there is space for laughter and warmth.

ROCKETMAN IN REAL LIFE? BETWEEN FACT AND FICTION

In an age of 'alternative facts' and 'fake news', it strikes me that it behoves Christians to hold to as high a standard of truth as possible. The events of the coronavirus pandemic have shown the life-saving value of access to accurate, truthful information. At the same time, we are not called to be like Gradgrind in Dickens' *Hard Times,* a man who is so obsessed with facts that he crushes the spirit out of the children he is supposed to teach. A poverty of imagination can be as devastating as poverty in food and shelter. One of the most powerful dimensions of works of fiction is their capacity to tell a deeper truth.

Rocketman is that tricky sort of film: the biopic. It must be recognised as fiction. For example, Taron Egerton puts in an amazing turn as Elton John, but it is *just* a turn. Equally, as someone who has written a memoir, I know only too well that to tell a story well, truthfully and economically requires sometimes ruthless decision-making.[2] The story of any life is never merely a list of facts. I think these pressures especially come into

---

[2] See Rachel Mann, *Dazzling Darkness: Gender, Sexuality, Illness and God*, Second Edition (Glasgow: Wild Goose, 2020).

play when a film about a living person is made. I don't think *Rocketman* escapes these issues. It is worth noting that it was made with the support of Sir Elton and, as a living subject, the content will necessarily be carefully vetted.

Is this a recipe for hagiography? Potentially. However, one of the things which makes *Rocketman* both brilliantly entertaining and so fascinating is Elton's willingness to expose his excessive and self-destructive behaviour to public scrutiny. Yes, it is ultimately a story of redemption and, in the closing credits, presents his later life as a series of triumphs. Given the ups-and-downs of his early life, this is hardly unreasonable. Elton's autobiography *Me* is just as candid and entertaining as the film. He does not pull any punches about his fruity life and, in an age of celebrity fakery, this makes him an endearing figure.

Any biopic should, nonetheless, be approached with caution, especially an authorised one. The film's decision to structure Elton's story through his songs is a sign of artistic license. This doesn't mean that the film is untrustworthy. It is worth noting that, in addition to Elton, the film includes a good number of people who (at the time of writing) are still alive, including his friend and co-writer Bernie Taupin. Inevitably, details will have been changed and events parsed together. What matters in this film is whether the decisions it makes tell the truth more intensely and thereby can take us deeper into the vagaries and beauties of the human condition. In this regard I feel *Rocketman* is an immense success. What it captures is a series of powerful moods and emotions that are eminently relatable. From the repressed post-War world into which Elton AKA Reggie Dwight was born through to the technicolour 1950s and the lurid excesses of the 1970s and 1980s, *Rocketman* is a broad-brush, wild ride. Given who Elton was and is this seems totally appropriate.

Whatever the final facts and wild fictions of *Rocketman* it is its underlying humanity that I think we should find enchanting and trustworthy. Elton is such a big character that the version of him contained in the film bears truth. There is charm, warmth, immense talent and profound vulnerability in his personality. One can readily see how the pre-sober Elton could drive people to exasperation. Yet, this fragility and need, as it turns towards self-awareness, is deeply human. It is a story to which many of us can relate. It will certainly be a story which we will have encountered. It is a story of redemption. It is a story we are invited to make in our own way in our Christian pilgrimage. It is a story of Lent.

WEEK 1

'In Want of Love' –
how do we become who we are?

TO START YOU THINKING

I have always considered myself a pretty resilient person. Perhaps that's because I've had to negotiate a fair few ups and downs. I've generally seen those ups and downs as having a powerful side-effect: the formation of character. Well, these days, I'm not so sure. Don't get me wrong. There is a lot to be said for having survived or come through times of trial. In the midst of them we can discover much more about who we are. However, one of the (ultimately positive) things that the Coronavirus 'Lockdown' of 2020 revealed to me is that I'm not quite so solid and independent as I like think I am. For, like many, I had to spend months in isolation. While I had the privilege of spending lockdown (and a fair amount of time either side) in a lovely rectory, I did so alone. I was not allowed to go out to the supermarket. Friends would drop off food and sometimes have a socially-distanced chat, but I was essentially cut off. After months of this I felt desperately deprived of human connection and warmth. I remember one day, after nearly three months without physical touch, a cat walked into my house. I reached down and it let me stroke it. My hands were shaking as the cat purred warmly. I almost cried.

We, as a species and as individuals, are made for love. I know that 'love' is one of the most overused words in the English language and always runs the risk of being twisted out of shape by misuse and a lack of precision. In English, one word is used too often to describe everything from romance, to friendship, to good familial relations, to sex and beyond. Love, as a word, can be adapted to almost every situation. Inevitably, this always risks making its use open to question. Too often, the word has been deployed to manipulate, convince and cajole others. Abusers and manipulators have used the word to get their own way. The sentence 'I love you' has powerful positive associations, but it has been used by the controlling and abusive to damage the lives of the vulnerable, too.

What my time in lockdown definitively revealed to me is that love is always a relational matter. It signals we are communal and social beings first. We are in the hands of each other, sometimes quite literally. I am not and probably never will be a 'touchy-feely' sort of person. Like many Brits who grew up in households without extravagant public display, I had to learn the power of hugs as a grown-up. Nonetheless, I am inclined to suggest that we are almost hard-wired for physical affirmation and connection. This goes back to our earliest embodied realities: as a species, we produce new-borns who can't look after themselves for a very long time. The human baby is practically the most defenceless and vulnerable creature on the planet. It depends for its flourishing and success on the love, care and cherishing of others. In short, it depends on a practical, relational love.

One of the wonders of God is that there is relationship at the heart of God's being. For all its bewildering mystery and – for some – offensiveness, the glory of the Triune God, of the Trinity, is the relationship inscribed in the Divine being from the beginning. Father, Son and Holy Spirit delight in their in-dwelling. This indwelling is sometimes called perichoresis – the dance of love at the heart of God. However, in those three Persons is absolute Oneness of Love. This is relationship as both perfection and as a signal of that towards which we are called.

If that is all too 'high faluting' and conceptual,

perhaps we should consider God as encountered in Jesus Christ. This is God who, as St Paul reminds us in Philippians 2, empties himself into the world as one of us. God comes among us not as power from on high or power over others, but as a babe in arms. He comes as one who is utterly dependent on the love of others. He comes as one with only one 'superpower': to call forth love and care from those who care for him. God calls forth love from all of us. We are invited into a living, loving relationship with God.

The first session of *Still Standing* examines our hunger for love, relationship and flourishing through the prism of Elton's own desire for love and affection. The desire for affection, as we've already seen, is a profoundly human desire. Even as our own stories depart from Elton's I think we can relate to this desire. Elton was born into a post-war British world whose deprivations and limitations it can feel difficult to imagine now. The young Reggie Dwight's parents were formed in a world in which Britain was still a Great Power. They were shaped by the turbulent 1930s and the shattering effects of the Second World War. When Elton was born in 1947, Britain was living under the debilitating effects of rationing. The young Reggie came of age in the 1950s and 1960s, times that represented a consumer boom when a new more rebellious spirit – represented by rock and roll – was being born. Nonetheless, these were still, for many, emotionally repressed times. In *Rocketman* we see – in concentrated form – how much the young Reggie Dwight longed for affection and love and how its relative absence had a potent and not always positive effect on his life.

However, even when our longings for relationship, affection and connection are discouraged, love will find a way. We see this in Elton's case through his gifts and passion for music. Music provides the outlet where love – where God? – can get at him. For those of us of faith, we may wish to put Elton's encounter with music, which represents something bigger and richer than himself, down to the work of God. We may wish to speak about how God's Spirit flows through the world, even when God seems absent or frustrated. This session offers us a chance to reflect on how life presents blockages and frustrations in our personal and corporate longings for love, yet also can blow our minds with God's grace.

Most of all, Session 1 of *Still Standing* gives us an opportunity to reflect on and express our need for love, connection and affection. To return to the point I made at the beginning: I think the coronavirus pandemic has revealed both how much we are made for love and affection, as well as how much we long to express it. The rules of 'social distancing' with which many of us have lived during lockdown and beyond, remind us of this. In our 'deprivations' we may have cried out, like the young Reggie, 'When are you going to hug me?' The love of God and of neighbour can often feel far away. Nonetheless, it waits for us as we wait for it. God walks towards us with the promise of love, even (perhaps especially) in the disciplines of Lent.

PRAYER

God of Love,
whether we feel you are far-off
or closer than our own bones,
help us to trust in your compassion,
your grace and your abundance.
May we know your faithful Love
flowing in and through and between us.
Lead us ever deeper
into friendship, service and love;

open our minds and hearts
to your Way of Grace
through Christ our Lord. Amen.

Icebreaker

What – in your opinion – is the best thing about being an adult? And the worst? Why do you think this?

What – in your opinion – is the best thing about being a child? And the worst? Again, why do you hold that opinion?

WATCH

From the opening credits to 06.28: 'When are you going to hug me?'

At the beginning of the film, we encounter Elton at his very lowest. He is dressed for a show, wearing a bright orange jump suit and horns. He looks like an orange devil. (For the more imaginative it might even be said that in wearing orange – a colour associated in the USA with prisoners – he signals the depths of his imprisonment to his inner demons.) He is in terrible shape, dead-eyed and unshaven. He enters a room which we discover is set up for group therapy. When asked why he is there, he seems both desperate, and inclined to treat it cynically, and almost facetiously. He makes his confession, using a version of the classic Alcoholics Anonymous formula ('My name is … and I am addicted …'); but even at this stage he seems determined to show that he has done more 'wicked' things than anyone else.

Then the therapist asks him what he was like as a child. This seems to both challenge and perk him up. He sees himself as a child again. He says that his childhood was great, though it is not clear we should believe him. We are taken back via one of Elton's songs ('The Bitch is Back') to the 1950s. It is a vision which, initially, seems bright, hopeful and comforting. We rapidly discover, however, that behind the vibrant façade is a rather boring, conventional suburban life.

This is a world where affection is withheld. It is a world in which Elton struggles. We meet his parents and grandmother, and witness the genesis of his talent. Elton especially wants love from his father, but he is spurned. We witness the depth of Elton's longing for affection as he asks, 'When are you going to hug me?' In the scene with which we begin *Still Standing* we witness the gap between Elton the 'wrecked adult' and Elton the 'promising child'.

Think about
What, if anything, strikes you about the scene you've just watched? Why?

Who, if anyone, shows love in this scene? How? What kind/s of love is demonstrated in this scene?

Are there elements of Elton's childhood you can relate to? Is there a difference between the experience of being a single child as opposed to growing up in a larger family unit?

In his poem 'This be the Verse', Philip Larkin suggests that parents mess children up (though he puts it a little more bluntly than that!).[3] What are the elements in his childhood that mess Elton up? What, if anything does this scene reveal about the power of good parenting?

What are the things in childhood that helped you become the person you are today? What damaged you or got in the way of your flourishing?

What place has God's parenting nurture had in your story?

In a time when people have lived with social-distancing, can you sympathise or empathise with Elton's longing for touch and hugs?

---

[3] The poem may be accessed here: https://www.poetryfoundation.org/poems/48419/this-be-the-verse

GOING DEEPER

Read
Luke 2:41-52

Luke 2 provides the single reference in the Gospels to the childhood of Jesus (as opposed to his infancy or nativity). At one level, it is a story about the gap between parental and childhood visions of responsibility. Anyone who has ever been a parent or exercised parental responsibility will surely have encountered this gap: parent or guardian expect one thing of a child and the child expects something else! To put it in a very basic, impious way, it's 'Please tidy your room!' versus 'But, mum, I'm busy playing X-box'.

Luke's story from Jesus' childhood takes this basic distinction between parental and childish pictures of responsibility to a quite different level. Mary and Joseph are travelling home after visiting Jerusalem for Passover, when they realise Jesus is not with them. They've gone a full day's journey before realising.

They rush back, no doubt in a panic, their imaginations full of the worst parental nightmares. What do they discover? Their twelve-year-old son in the Temple, teaching grown adults about God and the Scriptures. His parents are astonished and angry. They ask Jesus why he has treated them like this, to which he responds, 'Did you not know that I'd be in my Father's House?'

How does this passage both connect and contrast with what we've witnessed in the preceding scene from *Rocketman*?

To what extent are Mary and Joseph's reactions understandable? At a human level, have you ever been in a situation where you have lost someone for whom you bear responsibility? How did you respond?

What would you say to someone who claimed that

Jesus' behaviour is infuriating and that of a precocious child (rather like Elton!)? What would be your reaction if you were Jesus' parents?

What kind of pictures of parental love are shown in this passage? Are Mary and Joseph 'bad' parents for losing sight of their son? What do we make of Jesus' rebuke to his earthly parents? (Note: If anyone wonders why Jesus' parents could be so negligent, it is commonly claimed that pilgrimages during that period would have been undertaken as part of caravans; children would have been cared for communally.)

If we took the parenting of our Heavenly Father/ Parent seriously, what difference would it make in how we live our lives and our longing for love?

WATCH

From 08.30 to 15.00: 'Reggie's fantasy of love'

In this clip, we witness how Elton takes flight from the lack of affection shown by his parents into musical fantasy. We see how, as a small child, he discovers affirmation in music, as he both conducts and plays for an appreciative audience. We get a glimpse of his instinctive, natural gift, in which his 'ear for music' will provide the means of his 'salvation'. He is given an opportunity to study at the Royal College of Music, something about which he is terrified. His parents continue to marginalise him and police his behaviour, but his grandmother enables him to take up his scholarship. He impresses at his audition and is set on an exciting path. We gain further insight into his sterile family life as he and his family sing about their need for love and what prevents each of them from encountering it.

Given his experience with his parents, how reasonable is it that Elton 'escapes' into fantasy? Have you ever done something similar? Why?

To what extent do you think that Elton's gifts are 'nurtured' by his parents' lack of attention and affection?

Who, if anyone, models nurture and (divine) love in this scene?

Elton is an 'only child'. It is sometimes said that an 'only child' develops a capacity for independence and imagination that those with siblings do not? In your experience, is there any truth in this?

During the song, 'I Want Love', we begin to get a better sense of the inner struggles of Elton's parents and grandmother. The father, for example, implies perhaps that he might be suffering from post-traumatic stress disorder (PTSD). Should this make us more sympathetic to him and the others with parental responsibility? For what kind of love do they long?

GOING DEEPER

READ
1 John 4:7-21

The letters of John are among the most remarkable documents in the biblical canon. Traditionally attributed to John, the son of Zebedee, their exact authorship has been much discussed. It is certainly the case that the letters have an affinity with the language of John's Gospel. Contextually, the writer seems to be speaking against those in the emergent Christian community who have stepped away from the faith and have become convinced of their perfection and freedom from the requirements of God's laws. Ultimately, the faithful Christian community is exhorted to keep the Commandments of God. This, in essence, is the call to love God wholeheartedly and love one another in fullness. Love is practical, grounded and real and, most of all, the place where God's reality is revealed.

What are your initial reactions to the picture of love represented in this passage?

What gets in the way of us living out the life of love shown in this passage? What is the nearest we can get to experiencing this sort of love?

What might you say to someone who says that God

is not just Love, but so much more? What is the picture of love being unfolded in this passage? Does the love presented in the passage hold horizons of justice and peace and resistance in it?

WATCH

From 21:44 (Chapter Five) to 26.00: 'Becoming Elton'

In this scene we witness the young adult Reg Dwight, in the early stages of his musical career in the late 1960s, playing with the backing band, Bluesology. We begin to see the future Elton both flourish as a jobbing musician and explore his sexuality in the permissive, rough and tumble world of soul music. On tour, he asks an established soul man how 'a fat boy from Pinner' becomes a 'Soul Man'. First he is told to write some songs. Then the soul artist, who has clearly faced a lot of prejudice and barriers, dispenses this advice: 'You gotta kill the person you were born to be to become the person you want to be.' It is the prompt for Reggie to begin trying on identities and names. Finally, we see Reggie make his first steps as Elton John as he shares his piano work with the assistant to the major agent Dick James. We witness how he deals with his limitations: he's a great musician, with an instinctive ear for melody (he improvises the tune to 'Candle in the Wind'!), but he has no gift for writing lyrics.

The claim that you have to kill who you were born to be in order to become the person you want to be is very striking. To what extent to do you agree or disagree with it? Why? Is the soul artist more of a father to Elton than his own birth father?

To what extent is experimenting with our identities part of ordinary growing up? Do you think Elton – growing up in a homophobic world – faced particular pressures on being his true self? Did being playful about his identity help him cope in a prejudiced world?

As a young person – living with being trans – I felt great pressure to fit in with convention and conceal my identity. Simultaneously, I felt a strong inner need, welling up within me, to find ways to express myself and challenge convention. Have you or anyone you're close to lived through that tension? What is it like?

What do you think of the scene where Elton finally arrives at his name?

GOING DEEPER

Read
1 Corinthians 13

This is one of, if not the, most famous and well-beloved passages in the Bible. It is a fixture at weddings and at many funerals too. I have long considered it one of the 'self-validating' sections of the Bible. That is, it is a chapter of such transporting power that it indicates the abiding truth and power of Scripture. It presents a vision of the abiding power of love, a vision which (in my view) can speak into any person's life, whether they are religious or not. It reminds us that we may 'possess' any number of things – from wealth and material artefacts to remarkable gifts and power – but without love we are nothing. It reminds us that in this life we gain glimpses of glory, but we do not yet have the full picture of God's abundant love. Nonetheless, if we see through a mirror dimly now, we can be assured that faith, hope and love abide, and the greatest of these is love.

Why do you think this passage has become such a

classic at weddings and, in recent years, at funerals?
Does it deserve to be heard in other contexts more often?
If so, which?

Are there particular sections which leap out at you?
Why? Spend some time discussing these sections in the
group.

The passage is beautiful, mysterious and transporting.
How can it be translated into practice in everyday life?
What might a human life – Elton John's, or our own –
look like if we actually sought to live out this passage?

LOOKING AHEAD ...
ACTIVITIES TO
CONSIDER THIS WEEK

Hopefully this week's session has given you some resources through which to reflect, not only on the varieties of and necessity for love, but how the presence or absence of love can have a powerful impact on the formation of our character. As so often, it is only in hindsight that we see how God is at work in the particular moments of our lives. We see how love, or its absence, has been formative for our growth into the people we become.

I've long believed that God's defining and liberating love is available at any point or circumstance of one's life. Whether, like Elton, one has not had the most affectionate childhood or one has been lavished with hugs and kindness, God is available to help us grow ever more into the likeness of Christ. Though God doesn't promise us an easy ride, he promises to be with us till the end of the age.

One way of growing into this way of being open to God's love is by cultivating thankfulness. This is not always easy. I've experienced many tough times, and I know that it can be very difficult to be thankful. There are times in our lives when all we can do is wait, perhaps holding on by the thinnest thread. I'm not suggesting that one should be thankful for dreadful times or experiences. However, if the whole of life is – as I believe – a gift from God, it means that God remains present even in the roughest situations. This presence is a cause for thankfulness. Sitting and waiting, or crying out, in the pain can, strangely, be a form of thankfulness.

So perhaps this week, attempt to take a time each day to find something or some things for which you are thankful. It is a powerful way, in the midst of a very difficult world, to be alert to the love God has lavished and is lavishing on the universe.

CLOSING PRAYER

God of All,
you make each of us in love and for love.
May we have the boldness
to receive your lavish delight
with confidence and joy.
Teach us not only to know
we are loved, but accept
we are liked and cherished.
Help us to cherish those whom
we are called to serve. Amen.

WEEK 2

'Border Songs' – the power and price of friendship

TO START YOU THINKING

The poet and priest John Donne famously claimed that 'No man is an island, entire of itself.' By contrast, the songwriter Paul Simon, in a famous song, suggested that he was definitely a rock and an island! It would be interesting to see where each of us fits into the pictures Donne and Simon, respectively, sketch for us. Island or not? Donne – who goes on to say that 'every man is a piece of the continent, a part of the main' – wants to remind us that no one is above and beyond the community. We are always part of something larger, which is incomplete without us. Simon, by contrast, writing in the turbulent 1960s expresses the human need for distinctiveness and personal identity. Perhaps this is unsurprising: the 1960s was a decade when there was an opening up of free expression and personal choice after the conformist 1950s. Simon's song is a reminder of the existential wrestling many of us feel when we reflect on our inner lives. Much as Donne is right to suggest that we are all part of something greater than ourselves, it is true that society and community can be oppressive, denying oxygen to those who are different. Conformity can be deeply unpleasant.

In this week's *Still Standing* session I want to invite us to consider the power of friendship. It is one of my most extraordinary relationships in the world. Friendship can be a dimension of any relationship, from business through to familial and spousal and professional relationships. Friendship, I believe, can lead us into dreadful places as much as holy ones. For it can stop us from engaging our full moral judgment. Thus, for example, how often has it been said, when someone is exposed as an exploiter or abuser, 'But I never saw that. They were my friend. They were just so lovely and nice to me.' Friendship can get in the way of seeing a person clearly. At the same time, it provides beautiful connective tissue between people. I know that I would not be the person I am today without friendship. I like to think others would not have flourished without the friendship I have offered them.

I guess I am saying that I have long been convinced that Donne's claim – made suitably inclusive – is true. None of us is an island; each of us is part of something richer. In short, we are communal creatures first and individuals later. From the outset, the human baby is dependent on relationship and the care of others for nourishment. While it is true that distinctive personalities emerge as we grow older, few if any of us could truly flourish without the comfort and challenge of friendship. Friendship grounds us, shapes us and sets us free.

This week's session looks at the power and, indeed, the cost of friendship in *Rocketman*. For every strong and real friendship Elton forms, we see how he makes fake and unpleasant ones. For Elton, as much as for anyone, there are friendships and relationships that are not all they seem. These fake friendships expose him to exploitation.

At the core of *Rocketman* is Elton's friendship with Bernie Taupin. As we shall see, it is a proper friendship precisely because it is tested by circumstance and grounded in mutual love and respect. Set alongside that true friendship is the bleaker story of Elton's relationship with John Reid, the music manager, which promises so much but can never be equal. Later in the film, we also encounter Elton's relationship with his wife Renate, which he admits was broken from the start. As Elton acknowledges in the film, Renate did not deserve to be treated in the way she was.

Behind this talk of tested and fake friendship lies a vast biblical corpus which speaks powerfully into our modern narratives of friendship, love and loneliness. The Bible provides some striking ways of talking about friendship. In Biblical Hebrew, words like *reeh* and *oheb* have implications of 'friend' and 'one who loves' respectively. In the New Testament, Greek words like *philos* (friend), *hetairos* (companion) and *plesion* (neighbour) are used. There are a variety of strengths of relationship implied when these varied terms are used, including *adelphos*, which can mean 'brother/sister' in a filial, as well as fellow believer, sense.

As in English, the biblical terms for 'friend' hold a whole range of meanings. When, in Matthew 26:50, Jesus says to Judas at the Last Supper, 'Friend, do what you have to do', he speaks of Judas as companion. In English, we hear the potency of betrayal, which may take us to our own private and deeply personal encounters with the breakdown of friendships. However, this scene arguably has slightly different implications – that of an old comrade-in-arms turning on his friend. The betrayal is real, but not necessarily as intimate as we might think.

There are, in the Bible, friendships which absolutely go to the next level. Consider David and Jonathan in the First Book of Samuel. This is friendship which is not simply companionable or grounded in loyalty, but one which holds deep and genuine affection.[4] The friendship between David and Jonathan (and to a certain extent, Ruth and Naomi in Judges) has been coded as so loving and affectionate that it has been held up as a

---

[4] This contrasts with the sense of 'friendship' that a subject might be expected to offer to his or her monarch. See, for example, how Elizabeth calls Walsingham (her spymaster) her 'loyal friend' in the film, *Elizabeth: The Golden Age*.

model for same-gender love. For some LGBT+ people, David and Jonathan's love is iconic. They model not only companionship and loyalty, but affection too. Lest anyone think this kind of friendship is reserved for individuals, arguably St Paul demonstrates the same level of friendship for the Church at Philippi, in his Letter to the Philippians.

Our individual and corporate friendships with Christ has been the subject of some powerful hymnody. The famous hymn, 'What A Friend We Have in Jesus' explores our friendship with Jesus in a pretty direct manner. Written in the 1850s by preacher Joseph M. Scriven to comfort his mother (when she was living in Ireland and he in Canada), 'What A Friend' is too plangent and sentimental for some. However, its words remind us that friendship with Christ is of the deepest and most resilient kind. When Scriven asks, 'Can we find a friend so faithful/who will all our sorrows share?', he asks it rhetorically. For Christ is our loyal, affectionate and generous friend, who knows our travails and glories from the inside: 'Jesus knows our every weakness;/take it to the Lord in prayer!'

As we shall explore in this week's session, friendship is one of the glories of being human. It is a marker of the truth that we bear the image of God. While it certainly is something that can so readily go awry, that does not make it any less valuable. Perhaps it only adds to its significance. The Bible, and the book of Proverbs in particular, contains many comments on the fraught nature of friendship. In Proverbs 19:4, the writer says, 'Wealth attracts many friends, but even the closest friend of the poor person deserts them.' It is a comment on the toughness of life. However, for those alert to Jesus' death as a poor person persecuted and killed on a criminal's cross, it also serves as a reminder that Jesus' closest friends were inclined to desert him. Nonetheless, Jesus loved them and modelled true friendship. If, as I believe,

we are called into the likeness of Christ, Jesus' capacity
to show love in friendship under the toughest conditions
is an inspiration for us to do the same.

PRAYER

Living God,
you make us in and for relationship;
by your grace and encouragement,
help us to grow into your likeness.
Lead us, into rich, real and holy friendship
with our neighbours and most of all
with you, who is our true friend,
through your Son, our Saviour
Jesus Christ. Amen.

Icebreaker

In your experience, can the friendships we make provide
things that family relationships cannot or do not?

What is the most formative friendship you've had?
Why?

What effects can a bad friendship have?

What does a bad friend get up to?

WATCH

Chapter 5, from 26.18 to 30.38 – 'The Magic Envelope and Border Songs'

In this scene, we meet Bernie for the first time. In some ways, Bernie and Elton are very similar: they are ambitious, but lack confidence. They both still live at home and have not yet lost a youthful capacity to enjoy a moment of silliness, as shown when they sing, 'The Streets of Laredo'. There is something endearing about two people who *want* to be cool, but are very far from being so. However, they are also both gifted, able to bring the best out of each other. As they begin to bond, we hear the first single from Elton's eponymous 1970 album, *Border Song*. The lyrics, in part, capture Bernie's sense of alienation from London. It is also a rare collaboration in which Elton supplies the words for the final verse, a rejection of bigotry.[5] Two souls a little lost find each other, and in friendship begin to make their way in the world.

What makes for a good friendship?

What do we see in this scene which sets the basis for a strong friendship between Elton and Bernie?

Should we be less afraid of being uncool or geeky when we meet new people? Or is it wiser to be more 'defended'? Are there advantages in being open?

[5] The lyrics can be found here: https://genius.com/Elton-john-border-song-lyrics

Elton and Bernie bond over music and coffee. Elton also reveals his birth-name and is not judged by Bernie. They like to buzz over words and ideas. Do men and women typically bond differently to each other? Or are these gender differences in friendships overrated? What are your experiences?

To what extent does good friendship involve bringing the best out of each other? What is your experience of playing different, complementary roles in a friendship?

GOING DEEPER

Read
John 15:12-17

Jesus' words in this section of John's gospel are especially poignant. They are part of the section traditionally known as the Farewell Speeches, those words Jesus shares with his closest circle ahead of his arrest, trial, and crucifixion. They are shared in the context of John's account of the night during which Jesus shared his Last Supper with his inner circle. In John's version, the central focus is on Jesus' willingness to wash the feet of his disciples (John 13:1-17). Jesus says to Peter, 'If I do not wash you, you have no share with me'. Into this broad context, Jesus says to his followers, 'This is my commandment, that you love one another as I have loved you. No one has greater love than to lay down his life for his friends. You are my friends if you do what I command you.'

What is your initial response to this famous passage? (If it is easier, discuss in twos or threes before sharing with the wider group.)

What does it mean for Jesus to call us friend? Dare we call him friend? What are the implications for us if we call Jesus our friend?

Not everyone feels they have a close relationship with God, and, in different seasons, we may feel far away or close to God. How might each of us draw closer to God? What has helped you?

Is it always wrong or a bad sign to feel like God is far away? Can a time of dryness or 'darkness' be formative? (Perhaps, if you don't know it, look up the story of John of the Cross's 'Long Dark Night of the Soul'.)

WATCH

Chapter 7 (32.57 to 36.55) – 'The Soul Club'

In this scene, we see Elton and Bernie's friendship face its first real test: the disclosure that Elton is gay. As Elton and Bernie relax with friends from the Soul Scene, Elton is 'outed' by a gay soul singer. Bernie has made assumptions about who Elton is, based in part on the fact that Elton has a girlfriend. We witness Elton's anxiety and lack of confidence about who is he. Bernie is, seemingly, clearer minded. Elton asks if Bernie would be upset if Elton was gay. Bernie says he doesn't mind, though Elton's girlfriend might! When Elton later makes a pass at him, Bernie reminds Elton of the varieties of love: he says that he loves Elton, but not in that way.

In a profoundly homophobic culture like 1960s England, is Bernie's response to finding out about Elton's sexuality worthy of praise or is it surprising? Is the outing of Elton by his friend from the soul band understandable (given the costs of being gay at that time) or completely out of order?

What do you make of Bernie's acknowledgement that he loves Elton, but not in a sexual or romantic way? What kinds of love are there? To what extent does our society have an impoverished idea about love and friendship? Has it been impoverished by heterosexual and patriarchal ideas of love and relationship?

What do Elton and Bernie learn about the nature and

shape of friendship in this scene? What can it teach us about our friendships, if anything?

GOING DEEPER

Read
1 Samuel 18:1-5 (If time permits you may wish to read, in addition, 1 Samuel 20, especially verses 41-42, or 2 Samuel 1:25-27)

The friendship between David, the shepherd who becomes king, and Jonathan, the son of Saul, is one of the most remarkable in the Bible. There is a depth and intensity, and emotional congruence in their friendship which some in the modern world may find surprising. It is worth saying, that intense, emotive and intimate relationships between men – not necessarily coded as sexual – were part of the fabric of the ancient world. Indeed, in some ways the relationship between David and Jonathan, forged out of martial comradeship, is an analogue of the classical world's most famous male friendship: Achilles and Patroclus. Indeed, in *The Iliad*, Patroclus goes into battle against the Trojans wearing Achilles' armour (and is killed).

If, in repressed modern patriarchal societies, there can be suspicion when men weep tears, this is not the case in the Ancient world. Emotion and masculinity had not been disconnected. Extraordinarily, what we find between Jonathan and David is the use of 'covenant' language. This is no mere companionate friendship, but one built on promises. It is one which is tested and deepens through time. Whether we code their friendship as an icon of biblical representations of gay relationships or as a signal of what friendship might be at its deepest (without erotic or romantic dimensions), here is a relationship which invites awe and wonder.

What do you understand by the word 'covenant'? Are you surprised that it can be used in the context of friendship? Or should it be used more often? (Perhaps consider the concept of 'personal covenant' alongside other examples of biblical covenant.)

Are you surprised by the intimacy and mutual trust between Jonathan and David? If so, why? Do they offer a model for friendship in our times? Do they offer a critique of what is sometimes called 'toxic masculinity'?

How does living through a time of coronavirus pandemic affect our readings of the intimacy of David and Jonathan's friendship (or any friendship represented in the Bible)? Would you consider using the language of covenant for your friendships or particular friendships?

WATCH

Chapter 11 (58.15 – 1.03.28) – 'What do you want?'

John Reid was one of the most powerful music managers of the 1970s. He is sufficiently famous (some might say, 'notorious'!) that he also features in the film, *Bohemian Rhapsody*, as Freddie Mercury's personal manager. There he is portrayed as a toxic presence. Equally, in *Rocketman*, Reid is clearly presented as toxic. One of the fascinating things about Reid is how, in the garish world of Seventies rock and roll, he is presented as a strait-laced businessman. Indeed, in one sense, he is exactly who he says he is: a manager, who keeps his eye on the business. However, while Elton falls for Reid, the latter retains a careful, almost cruel distance. As their relationship develops, Reid is portrayed as ever more manipulative, controlling and calculating. At one point, he even suggests that he needs to find a girlfriend for Elton as cover (what is sometimes called in the gay community, a 'beard'). Elton imagines he can trust Reid, but Reid – as portrayed in the film – betrays and exploits him until he is worth as much to Reid dead as he is alive.

What is it about Reid that Elton finds appealing and attractive? Should he have seen through him earlier?

How can we ensure that our friendships remain places where we are safe and flourish? Can we? What kinds of filters do you use when forming friendships?

Are we more likely to end up in toxic relationships in our youth or is that claim wrong?

Is there a sense in which Reid is entirely honest with Elton? He is, after all, precisely who he presents himself as: a business manager. What would you say to someone who said it was Elton's fault that he got in the mess he did?

When Reid suggests that Elton finds a girlfriend as 'cover', how do you react? Is this a reasonable strategy for a celebrity to adopt in a homophobic world or is Reid simply protecting his financial interests?

GOING DEEPER

Read

Matthew 26:14-25 (Should you wish to explore an alternative biblical story about poor friendship, do take a look at Genesis 40:1-23, the story of Joseph and Pharaoh's Cupbearer)

Is there a more famous story of betrayed friendship in world culture than Judas's betrayal of Jesus? It is something which, even in our post-Christian society, is known by most people, even if only via repeat productions and showings of *Jesus Christ Superstar*. While it would be verging on the absurd to compare John Reid's exploitation and betrayal of Elton with Judas's betrayal of Christ, Judas's story runs so deep in our culture that it's hard not to cast Reid as a 'Judas'. While there are people who claim that Judas has been cast as too much the villain of the piece – occupying in Dante's *Inferno*, the very lowest layer of hell – Judas' behaviour as portrayed in the Bible is striking: his behaviour is a signal of how readily relationships can sour, and how God himself, in the person of Christ, knows the cost of broken friendship.

It is a moment of shock and a profound human tragedy.

Has Judas been given a raw deal by Christians? Why? If not, why not?

In Matthew's account, it is clear that Jesus is aware of Judas's betrayal. Why, in your view, does Jesus permit Judas to stay at the Last Supper and receive broken bread and wine outpoured?

Would you permit someone who was about to betray you to share food and fellowship with you?

Can someone like Judas be redeemed or is such a person – as in the image of Dante's *Inferno* – doomed to be beyond the comfort of God?

If you've been betrayed (or you have betrayed the trust of another), has forgiveness been possible? What, if anything, has made reconciliation possible?

LOOKING AHEAD ...
ACTIVITIES TO
CONSIDER THIS WEEK

Reconciliation is one of the most profound works of God. Indeed, arguably Christ's work of redemption is nothing more nor less than the work of grace that reconciles God to humanity. In our personal, private and communal lives, we are clearly not called to be Christ. However, we continue to participate in his work of redemption when we become people and communities of reconciliation.

This week, then, if it is possible, each of us might look out for opportunities for reconciliation – with individuals and communities, and indeed with the wider world. There are relationships that are toxic, and I am not for a second suggesting that anyone should place themselves in danger of abuse or further exploitation. However, there is a wider reality of relationships that may be improved through loving attention.

In a world where people are exploited and abused, this may also be the week in which to lend one's practical and financial support to organisations working to end the use and abuse of human beings. In light of recent high-profile #BlackLivesMatter campaigns, you may wish to lend practical and financial support to organisations which work to end racism. Reconciliation is, after all, surely predicated on justice.

Equally, one might want to investigate the work of reconciliation organisations like the Corrymeela Community, which has worked to heal the divide between Catholics and Protestants in Northern Ireland. Perhaps consider attending a service run by the Open Table Network which works to ensure that LGBT+ people have as strong a sense of home in the church as straight people.

CLOSING PRAYER

Living God,
we thank you that you came among us
as your Son, the Prince of Peace.
Enable us through your grace
to model the kind of reconciling love
shown by Christ
in the Garden of Resurrection.
Help us to follow the hard path
where justice and mercy is found
in the midst of ordinary human need. Amen.

WEEK 3

*'Into Orbit' – the temptations
and promises of 'success'*

TO START YOU THINKING

Whatever else we might believe about the career of Elton John there is one undeniable truth: he has been colossally, globally successful. I think it was Humphrey Bogart who said that no Hollywood star is famous until he is famous on the streets of Delhi. His point: you're not famous until you're known outside of your national or cultural bubble. Elton is famous and successful around the planet and – as *Rocketman* makes clear – in the 1970s, he was basically the best-selling artist in the world.

I suspect that many people using this study guide will have had their fair share of 'glimpses of glory', amidst the chaff and challenges. However, our personal triumphs can seem to be very small beer when set alongside those of a global superstar. It can be very difficult to imagine what global, popular success looks like. In the late 1960s and into the 1970s, rock music offered a previously unimagined route to adoration and success for people from relatively humble backgrounds. A working-class or lower-middle class kid could go, within a few months, from living in a two-up, two-down to a mansion with Palladian flourishes and several Rolls Royces. The international roads opened up by the likes of The Beatles or The Rolling Stones meant that British kids like Elton could access the vast US and Japanese markets like never before.

Perhaps, because of the adulation showered on rock stars in the 1960s, it is unsurprising that comparisons between musicians and religious figures became commonplace. A musical like *Jesus Christ Superstar* became possible not only because of the emergence of high-powered amplification, but because Jesus could be read through a rock star lens, and vice versa. In 1974, *Stardust*, which featured David Essex as Jim MacLaine, looks at what happens to a working-class kid (a character first featured in 1973's *That'll Be The Day*) who becomes a major rock star, takes loads of drugs and begins to believe his own hype. He starts to see himself almost as a saviour figure.

While a life of global superstardom is very far from most people's personal experience, and arguably from the demands of grounded faith and religion, this does not make someone like Elton John unrelatable. As already indicated, there are few of us who have not had some encounter with success (and failure), in however modest a way. We have all had moments of triumph. Certainly, we have all witnessed the success of others and seen what it can do to them. I know few people who lack strong opinions about successful and immensely wealthy people.

It's fair to say that the Christian faith has, at best, an ambiguous relationship with what might be called 'worldly' success and wealth. While it is the case that, down the centuries, there have been a fair number of Christians who have held substantial fortunes, Jesus says things about wealth and worldly success which make his hearers uncomfortable. He famously suggests that one cannot serve both God and Money/Mammon (Matthew 6:24). He also invites us to know where our treasures lie. Indeed, each Ash Wednesday, one of the established lectionary texts is Matthew 6:19-20, in which we are invited to seek after treasure in heaven.

Being a Christian in a consumerist, money-driven world (in which our financial system seems to idolise 'wealth' and treat 'money' as a god) is always going to be interesting. Indeed, in the midst of Christ's injunction to store up treasure in heaven, there is a profound sense in which the Christian faith is seriously 'this-worldly'. I think there is a very strong case for saying that being a Christian requires us to be profoundly attentive to the world in which we live now. The repeated effects of financial crises, austerity and the coronavirus pandemic reveal the profound divisions in our societies. We are not 'all in this together' in the same way. Equally, cultural 'moments' like Black Lives Matter and #MeToo reveal that our world is profoundly inequitable and marked by stains of privilege and prejudice. We do not need to be fully paid up Liberation Theologians, who believe that God has a preferential option for the excluded, to know that how we live in this life matters to our Christian formation and character.

I guess I am saying that being Christian does have implications for how we live in this world. It is not simply a matter of saying 'I believe X' and then never bearing fruit in holy or gracious action. During the protests that followed the murder of George Floyd, the widespread and justified condemnation of President Donald Trump's use of the Bible as a prop reveals how calling oneself a Christian is not the same as being one.

However, Christians always risk coming across as priggish or supercilious should we become too critical or suspicious of public success or personal achievement. A righteous desire to work for the relief of the pain of the many can become a slightly sneery dismissal of those who have achieved a measure of worldly success or financial power. Quite where that line might be drawn probably depends on a Christian's temperament, theological or ecclesial tradition, and personal privilege. Clearly it is possible to become famous or make a lot of money (or both) and behave in a generous manner. For example, the Quaker Cadbury family made an enormous amount of money in the nineteenth century through their

Birmingham chocolate business. At the same time, they created Bournville Village for their workers, offering attractive homes which would have been beyond the means of most workers of the time.

This week's session of *Still Standing* offers a chance to enjoy the early successes of Elton as he becomes one of the world's first megastars. Those first moments of international fame are amazing. Indeed, one of the truly delightful highlights of the film is the way his career 'takes off' in the early 1970s. At the same time, we witness how success is not in itself a solution to his inner struggles. The promise of wealth, fame and adulation may meet some very particular needs – not least enabling him to live comfortably – but it is not the answer to the inner demons with which he struggles. If his wealth and power may seem far removed from the kinds of lives most of us lead, his response to fame is a very human story with which I suspect most people can relate. So often we act as if *only* we had this or that, or achieved this or that, then we would be happy or complete. Deep self-acceptance and peace is to be discovered elsewhere. As Christians, we claim that it is to be found in the company of the Living God.

PRAYER

Father God,
you invite us to embody holiness
by growing into the likeness of your Son.
Help us to seek after treasure in heaven,
and live wisely and generously on earth.
Grant us discernment and good judgment
so that we may be gracious and kind
to those whom we are called to serve and love.
Amen.

Icebreaker

Do you have strong opinions about success and wealth? Should Christians be comfortable with success and achievement in this world or not? Should Christians be suspicious of wealth? Why do you believe as you do?

WATCH

From the beginning of Chapter 4 to 21.44 – 'Saturday Night'

In this scene, we meet the young Reggie testing out his gifts in public for the first time. We witness the resistance to his classical gifts. However, when he springs into playing 'Saturday Night's Alright (For Fighting)' we see his stage confidence emerge. This is a young man learning to let go musically and find his place in the world. He enjoys the world for the first time. As a rock and roll fan and as a teenager he discovers a multi-dimensioned and multicultural world. In this scene, he claims space as he sings, 'I'm a juvenile product of the working class'. The world is alive and seems his for the taking for the very first time. It is at this point that his talent is spotted and he and his band are offered work as a backing band.

To what extent does this scene capture the energy and excitement of youth and going out into the world as a teenager and a young person? How does it connect and disconnect from your experience?

Do you remember how it felt to explore the world as a teenager for the first time? Was it a positive or negative experience?

How much does 'success' (however we define it!), depend on having the freedom and safety to test out one's skills, gifts and talents as a young person? Are we more likely to 'succeed' when we have a secure childhood in which we can take risks?

In our world, which can seem very different to Elton's, and which is marked by new opportunities and challenges (from coronavirus through to online culture), how can younger people be encouraged to find the confidence they need to be successful or believe in themselves? Or do they already possess confidence?

GOING DEEPER

Read
1 Samuel 17:4-15, 20-24, 32-50.

The story of David and Goliath is a classic 'Sunday School' story. It is sufficiently famous that it has become a cultural trope. One does not need to have attended church to have heard about 'David vs Goliath' stories in sport, politics and so on. It is a remarkable story and justly famous, whatever else we think about it. For here is the story of a young man, barely more than a boy, taking on the greatest warrior in the Philistine army and triumphing.

How does the biblical account of David vs Goliath compare to your memory of it, say, from Sunday School or what you might have picked up from the wider culture?

In one sense this is a story about how the less powerful can 'stand up' to those who hold power and threaten others. 'Less powerful' might include young people, global majority people, women, LGBTI people. Does the David and Goliath story speak into the stories of those who wish to 'claim' their power? Or does it present an unrealistic picture?

What do you make of the line in which David says to Goliath, 'You come against me with sword and spear and javelin, but I come against you in the name of the Lord Almighty, the God of the armies of Israel, whom you have defied'? What would it be like to claim the 'armour of God' for ourselves in our lives and struggles?

When people wish to claim a place in the world, or achieve success or find their voice, to what extent does it depend on toppling those more powerful or breaking the status quo? Or are there more equitable ways of bringing about change?

WATCH

38.01 through to 48.36: From private talent to public superstar

This is one of those pivotal scenes in *Rocketman*. We witness Elton transform Bernie's words into the absolutely classic *Your Song*, in real time. It is the moment their writing relationship is cemented, and Elton begins to find and own his voice. The scene moves from home to Elton as he records this song and receives acclaim from Dick James, who was notoriously hard to please. It is at this point that Elton comes to a crossroads: James wants him to sing at the world-famous *Troubadour Club* in Los Angeles, owned by Doug Weston.

Going to L.A. would be both a dream come true but also be a moment of 'threat': it represents the moment where Elton's voice, talent and performance will be put to the test in front of audiences that have judged, made, and also ruined some of the finest musicians in the rock world. Elton is terrified, but he has to take his chance to show the world who he is. As he meets Doug Weston, takes in the vibes of the Troubadour and, finally, after overcoming his stage-fright, wows the crowd with *Crocodile Rock*, 'Elton John Superstar' is truly born.

What strikes you about the scene we've just watched? How do you respond to Elton's lack of confidence?

Have you ever been in situations where you lacked public confidence? If so how did you address it, if at all? Sometimes is it okay to wear a mask or dress up in a costume to cope with a difficult situation? (That is, to hide some things about ourselves in order to show off?)

Apparently, Elton's real-life residency at the Troubadour Club was a sensation. Have you ever been to a gig, event or concert that has taken you 'into orbit'? What made it so amazing?

Is there something special about witnessing someone 'find their voice' for the first time? Have you ever had to find your voice or witnessed someone find their voice? What can an authentic voice achieve?

GOING DEEPER

Read
Exodus 4:1-17

The context for this reading is Moses' encounter with the Lord in the form of the Burning Bush (you might wish to read Exodus 3 in preparation for the session). Exodus 4, itself, is a fascinating exploration of Moses attempting to talk himself out of the mission the Living God wishes him to undertake: to lead the people of God out from Egypt into the promised land. Moses' reticence is surely understandable. Egypt was a superpower. How might any one person challenge its authority? Moses was, of course, also a fugitive from Egyptian justice. It is surely absurd for him to head back to the land where he has killed a man. God, however, equips Moses with what he needs. Moses will return to Egypt able to demonstrate God's power to transform a staff into a snake or Moses' healthy hand into a diseased one. Still, Moses tries to talk himself of the mission. He says he is not an eloquent man, and the Lord begins to lose patience with him. Finally, God sends Aaron along with Moses as his 'mouthpiece', and Moses agrees to take on his mission.

To what extent do you have sympathy or empathy with Moses in this section of Exodus? How would you feel if you were asked to 'face down' a world power on behalf of God? (Might you feel like Greta Thunberg at the UN?) With what 'gifts' would you want God to equip you?

Have you faced situations where you have felt ill-equipped? What are we being invited to speak up for or act for in the world today? What does God provide to help us act?

What does this scene reveal about how we might be in our relationship/s with God? Should we be bolder? What does it mean to 'find our voice' when speaking to/praying with God?

WATCH

Chapter 11 (55.10 through to 58.00) – Elton goes global, and Chapter 12 (1.06.15 to 1.11.42) – Elton under strain

After the success of the Troubadour gig, Elton goes stratospheric. He learns to love the attention and indulges in design and ever growing excess. We see how 'Elton Hercules John' becomes the biggest artist on the planet. Though Elton and Bernie both think this success can't last, the bandwagon rolls on and on.

In the second clip for this section we witness the implications of Elton's highlife unfold. We return to Elton in therapy, a broken man who feels utterly alone in a world where everyone supposedly loves him. He 'hulks out' and demands a drink. We then see Elton on the way to the Royal Variety Show when he decides to tell his mother he is gay (in part because his manager has told him to do so, for cover purposes). He receives a cold response from his mother, suggesting that Elton will never be loved. He is then abused and hit by Reid, before putting on his 'stage face' and entertaining the crowds once again.

In this scene, Elton says, 'Real love is hard to come by so you find a way to cope without it.' What do you make of that statement? How true have you found it to be?

Have you ever used props and crutches to cope? What

do you make of Bernie's challenge to Elton to simply go 'out there' and entertain without the 'paraphernalia'?

We see how Elton is 'loved' by millions in this scene, but what does he really need to be 'successful'?

What do you make of Elton's mother in this scene? And Reid? What has Elton lost and what does he need to find?

GOING DEEPER

Read
Psalm 86

The theologian Dietrich Bonhoeffer called the Psalms the prayer-book of Jesus Christ. I think he meant that these were the prayers with which Jesus would have grown up. Jesus would have known them so profoundly, they became the language of his deepest heart (we see this when Jesus prays words from Psalm 22 on the Cross, 'My God, why have you forgotten me?'). The Psalms have comforted and challenged countless millions. Psalm 86 is traditionally attributed to David. It is a psalm that asks for help, protection and comfort in a time of need. Whether it was 'written' by David when he was on the run and in fear for his life, or by someone else, is beside the point. Psalm 86 has enormous power to speak into our lives when we find ourselves in distress, compassed by enemies and the untrustworthy, and in need of comfort.

The Psalms were, until relatively recently in the Church of England, regularly chanted or sung. What is your relationship with the Psalms? Do you feel a strong connection with their moods and possibilities?

What do you make of Psalm 86. What, if anything, strikes you about it? (Perhaps spend a few minutes chatting with another participant about your reaction to it, then share with the group.)

To what extent does this psalm speak into the situation Elton faces in the scenes we've just watched?

What difference can praying a psalm like Psalm 86 when we face situations of pressure or distress? Is it simply cathartic or are there other things going on?

The speaker in Psalm 86 has a strong sense that bad people are out to get him. What do you make of the speaker's claim, in verse 17, that in being shown favour by God, his enemies will be put to shame? Is that just vengeful? Or something else? Is it a 'Christian' response to being under pressure and strain? Why do you think as you do?

LOOKING AHEAD ...
ACTIVITIES TO
CONSIDER THIS WEEK

Perhaps this coming week gives each of us an opportunity to adjust, just a little, the 'scope' through which we assess our lives. Have we been too obsessed with worldly success or the desire for money, beyond that which we need? Are we too inattentive to what is truly valuable? Depending on our answers to those kinds of questions, we may wish to look again at how we use our time, gifts and (depending on circumstance) financial power and privilege. What are the places where our gifts might best be deployed?

This week's session also invites reflection on 'finding a voice' and using our voices for good. One area where all of us might grow is in how we relate to, speak to and listen to God. Might we be bolder and more honest? Is it time to embrace silence and listen to what the still small voice of God actually has to say?

How we speak to each other matters too. Perhaps this week, each of us might pay especial attention to how we speak, write and relate to other people. For those of us who use social media, it is perhaps worth being attentive to how we frame our participation in those spaces. Am I being civil? Generous? Truthful? Do I respect the fact that the person I am addressing is still God's child?

CLOSING PRAYER

*O God, whose Spirit is the Breath of the Universe,
sing your song of love and grace through us!
Teach us when to speak and when to be silent,
when to act and when to be still.
In all we do, may we hold your Law of Love
before our hearts; call us to work
for justice, mercy and peace.
Through your Son, Jesus Christ our Lord. Amen.*

WEEK 4

*'Sad Situations' – when sorry is
the hardest word*

TO START YOU THINKING

German is a remarkable language. I had the good fortune to study it at school and, though I never even came close to mastering it, I was most impressed by its ability to capture a mood with precision. Sometimes it achieved this through its gift for 'compound words'. Words like *das Fernweh*, literally the 'distant ache', which indicates a longing to travel. Or *das kopfkino* or 'head-cinema', which refers to a phenomenon most of us know: our ability to play images in our heads. Perhaps the most famous compound word, certainly as an English 'loan word', is *(die) Schadenfreude*. It refers to the pleasure we can feel at other people's misfortunes. In German it literally means 'harm joy'.

Please don't judge me too harshly, but I have felt Schadenfreude when certain people have taken a bit of a fall. I am one of those people who, back in 1997, felt pleasure when Michael Portillo lost his parliamentary seat to Stephen Twigg. Since then, Portillo has acknowledged that given his political positions, notably on social issues, back in 1997, it is hardly unsurprising that many socially liberal people like me felt a rush of pleasure. Since then Portillo has reassessed some of his positions and has become something of a National Treasure. Indeed, when we were panellists on *The Moral Maze* together I was reminded that he – as much as any of us – is a human being.

The concept of a 'Fall From Grace' is an ancient one. The very first Fall is described in Genesis 2 and 3, when

– according to the old school reading – Eve gives in to the Serpent's wiles and persuades Adam, representing Humanity, to join her in feasting on Forbidden Fruit and messes up Paradise. It is a story with endless resonance and permits of a range of readings which go beyond the traditional. That is not the central focus here.[6] What is fascinating is how the concept of the Fall plays out not just at the 'global' level, as in the myth of Adam and Eve, but at every level of culture and society. I've already mentioned, via the example of Michael Portillo, the trope of the political fall from grace, but there are other familiar varieties. Certainly, there was a time, when the tabloid was king and Christianity was more prominent, that stories of priests and vicars caught in compromising situations could make the front page. Pleasure was taken in the fall of 'moral exemplars'.

We live, arguably, in a world where celebrity has never been more powerful. It is a world which Elton, through his talent and glamour, has helped create. This is a world which began to emerge in the excess of the 1970s. Tabloids and, since the turn of the millennium, the internet and social media have created 24-hour obsessions with the rise and fall of celebrities. If 'celebrity culture' has been fed massively in the past fifteen years, many of its features (money, glamour, excess, unaccountability, and an obsession with youth) have been part of popular western culture since the 1950s. Elton presents a powerful case study in what can happen to a gifted young man who is given everything without many of the skills or the inner awareness to cope with it.

This week's session provides an opportunity to witness Elton trapped between success and sadness.

[6] If you'd like to investigate alternative readings of the Eden myth, see classic works like Phyllis Trible's *God and the Rhetoric of Sexuality* (Indiana: Fortress 1978), among many others.

He might 'have it all' but he is falling ever deeper into his own personal hell. It is not an easy watch. This is a study in human decay. However, some might feel little empathy for Elton: as one of the wealthiest rock stars on the planet, perhaps some might respond by saying, 'So what? If he can't handle fame and fortune, that's his look-out?' I guess that is an understandable reaction. Elton's life is hardly one of poverty. Many who have difficult lives dream of having even a fraction of his wealth. It is understandable why people feel Schadenfreude when people like Elton take a fall. Perhaps, some might even understand why his struggles in the 1970s and 1980s caused so much interest in the tabloids.

What might count as a Christian response to the struggles and travails, the fall from grace, of another human being? That is the central focus of this week's study. In exploring Elton's raw and sometimes shocking encounter with the bleak possibilities of excess, I hope we can meet that with grace. Christ invites us to avoid judging others, lest we be judged, no matter how tempting. Some users of this book may feel that what is lacking from Elton's life, pre-rehab, was a lack of both appropriate self-love as well as discipline.

If Christianity has sometimes been suspicious of 'loving oneself', it remains a key part of Christ's summary of the Law. He s ays that we must love neighbour as we love ourselves. It is very easy, in our hunger to serve and love others, to forget to love ourselves. Clearly, in the depths of his fall, Elton was not driven by a desire to love his neighbour! However, neither was he in a position to love himself sufficiently so that he could love those around him appropriately.

Equally, when Christians speak of the importance of 'discipline' it sounds weird and inappropriate to the modern ear. It has implications of violence or correction. It has unpleasant connotations. Nonetheless, it has traction. When we talk about being 'disciples of Christ' we speak about people under discipline – who follow a teacher or a set of practices and rules. The rule of Love is, arguably, the highest law of Christ.

There is a discipline to love ... that is, love is never merely capricious or random. Love settles in the body and changes us. This, arguably, is the journey Elton is groping towards in this session of *Still Standing*. His journey is painful, difficult and real. It is a challenge to witness. As we see events unfold, we pray and hope he can get to where he ultimately needs to be – where Love can find him and call him into a new way of being.

PRAYER

God of Forgiveness and Grace,
we come before you
knowing that none of us
is as loving and generous
as we are called to be.
Break through our hardness
of heart and the poverty
of our spirit, with the riches
of your grace. Amen.

Icebreaker
How do you react when public figures or celebrities fall from grace? Can you think of an occasion when you felt pleasure? Or horror? Or disappointment? Why do notable or famous people produce powerful reactions in us?

WATCH

Chapter 14 (1.13.08 to 1.21.14): The Rocketman falls and rises again?

Elton is a bona fide megastar, with houses across the world. We meet him in his LA house, where he is exhausted and – for a relatively young man – starting to look careworn. His manager John Reid goes from strength to strength, effectively boasting about how important he is to Elton's career. Elton tries to point out that without him Reid is nothing, but it is clear that it is Elton who is out of control. At this point, Elton's grandmother, mum and step-dad arrive. He realises that he genuinely is lost and has no sense of time, value and space. As a party starts, and Bernie arrives with women on his arms, Elton feels still more out of it. He attempts to take his own life in the swimming pool. He encounters his younger self, and recognises how much he is alienated from that little boy. We see how Elton is saved from death, and effectively plugged back into the Rock and Roll Machine and forced to perform again.

'What a shy little boy you were. Look at you now,' says one of Elton's mother's friends. How do you feel witnessing this difficult and troubling scene? What stands out about it?

As indicated in the introduction, 'Schadenfreude' is a common emotion. Why do some people (all of us at different points), take pleasure in the fall and breakdown of others? Doesn't this scene expose why compassion is so crucial to loving community? Why do we struggle to show it?

In this scene, what is more monstrous: John Reid, who is all about the money, or the system that requires Elton to keep on performing for the sake of entertaining others? Or does Elton still get a buzz out of performance? (Look at his face as he receives the adulation of the crowd.)

'I'm not the man they think I am at home.' Have you ever had to negotiate the gap between what you feel in your own head and what others think of you? (For example, some people are surprised when I say that I spend a lot of time thinking that other people dislike me, even when they reassure me that I'm good and kind.)

GOING DEEPER

Read
Matthew 7:24-27 – The Wise and Foolish Builders

Whatever else people might dispute about Jesus, he was clearly a storyteller of genius. This simple parable – literally 'a throwing aside' or a juxtaposition – invites his audience to think on wisdom and what it means to listen to and obey the word of God. Jesus suggests that the person who does not hear his words and act on them is like a man who builds his house on sand; when storms come the house is washed away. The person who hears and acts is one who builds their house on rock, fit for the world's storms.

What, if anything, do you find striking in this parable?

Elton is a man who has everything. His world is built on the 'rock' of money, property and success. Why do they fail him? What would help him to be better positioned to negotiate the storms of life?

Can we be both like the foolish and wise builder at the same time? What are the things in your life that have seemed like they're built on rock only to founder in the storm?

Has the coronavirus pandemic and the emergent climate crisis invited each of us to 'rescope' on what it means to build our 'houses' on 'rock'? How have you responded to these situations?

WATCH

Chapter 15 (From 1.21.18 to 1.23.20mins) – Bernie and Elton part ways

Here we encounter Elton and Bernie having a private moment together, quite literally up in the clouds. Bernie is tired and worn-out. He tells Elton that he needs to go home and have a break. He can see that Elton is burnt-out too and suggests that he and Elton – the old pals from the beginning – disappear and write together as they used to. He says they should go home. But Elton can't break the cycle of touring yet. Unconvincingly, he says he wants to collaborate with other writers. We then see Elton on stage dressed as Queen Elizabeth I, so intoxicated he can't even remember where he is. The crowd boo and he tells people to go home if they aren't happy.

Are there things you find striking in this short scene? What does it reveal about the differences between Elton and Bernie? Who would you prefer to be at this point in the narrative?

Why does Elton struggle to listen to the invitation of his old friend? What is going on in Elton's head?

When Elton has a go at the crowd is he to be pitied or does he deserve to be booed? Or a little of both? Why do you answer as you do?

GOING DEEPER

Read
Luke 15:11-32: The Lost Son

This parable is so famous that it can seem as if there is nothing left to say about it. Part of its genius, however, is the way it holds endless resonances, readings and possibilities. Jesus doesn't tell us how to interpret it. He leaves it up to us. Clearly, given its usual title – the 'prodigal' or 'lost son' – we inevitably find our attention drawn to the character who leaves home, gets very lost and returns. However, the dynamics of this parable are much richer and deeper than that. Perhaps we need to learn to pay more attention to the father and the older son, as well as the relationships that inhere between the three main characters.

Given that Elton was an only child, you might feel that this parable doesn't really connect with his story. Or is that to limit the power of the parable? Is it possible for any person – with many siblings or none – to identify with the central characters at different times in their lives?

Do you feel more like the father, the older son or the 'lost' son? Can you think of situations when that has shifted or been different? What does it feel like to occupy those different 'positions' at different times?

What, for you, is the central motif or point of the parable? Why do you say that? Given what you believe about the parable, how might it speak into the stories of people like Elton (in the early Eighties) who had lost their way?

WATCH

Start of Chapter 16 (From 1.25.30 to 1.31.26): Elton truly lost …

Elton is now driven by addictions and, without Bernie, his music has suffered. John Reid taunts him and insists he will make money off of Elton whether he is alive or dead. We see Elton in the studio surrounded by sycophants, unconcerned by his distress. However, he is treated kindly by Renate Blauer, a recording engineer, and in desperation he reaches out to her. They find a connection and they marry. Though they are affectionate, the marriage lacks sustaining love and it cannot provide a solution to Elton's problems. The marriage rapidly falls apart. We finally see Elton back in therapy acknowledging that he treated Renate badly, dragging her into his madness.

How do you react to Elton's 'treatment' of Renate? Is he too harsh on himself? Why do you think what you do? After all, they are both adults.

Arguably, at this point in the narrative, Elton cannot see himself clearly. Can we ever see ourselves clearly or are we always doomed to see ourselves through a distorting mirror? What helps us grow more clear-sighted and less self-deceptive?

Have you ever been in a situation where you are surrounded by sycophants telling you your work is amazing, when you know it is not? How do we distinguish between false friends and 'courtiers' and true, proper friends?

If you had to choose, would you prefer people to praise you and tell you how great and amazing you are, or for people to be ruthlessly honest at all times? If you could only choose one, which would you go for? Why?

GOING DEEPER

Read
James 1:19-27

The Letter of James is traditionally attributed to James, the brother of Jesus, AKA 'James the Just.' Whether it was actually written by him is, in some ways, beside the point. It is often considered a curiosity because, famously, it has been read as overly focussed on 'works' – good action in the world – rather than on 'grace'. Early in his career, Martin Luther, the Reformer who has been most identified with doctrines of salvation by grace alone, suggested it should not be included in the Bible. It has been characterised as written for an audience of Jewish Christians. Whatever, we think of its 'backstory', it offers a determined reminder that how we are and how we act in the world matters to our relationship with God. In the passage we consider now, James suggests that those who are 'doers of the word' move clearer of self-deception than those who don't. Indeed, those who hear but do not act are like those who see themselves in a mirror, look away and promptly forget who they are.

What are your initial reactions on reading this section of scripture? Is there anything that surprises you? Anything you feel drawn to? Why?

This letter has sometimes been accused of displaying the 'British' or 'Pelagian' heresy. This is the heresy that humanity can achieve perfection without grace and by works alone (it is called the 'British Heresy' because Pelagius was born in Britain). Do you have any sympathy for the belief that we can be saved by good works alone? Why, if at all, is Pelagianism problematic?

What do you make of the claim that hearing and acting on the Word of God is a way of avoiding self-deception and remembering who we are? Is something more required to help us be our 'true' selves?

LOOKING AHEAD ...
ACTIVITIES TO
CONSIDER THIS WEEK

Jesus says, 'Love your neighbour as yourself.' Clearly it is important, then, to look outwards and seek to serve and build-up our neighbours. This week it is worth thinking and acting on that calling on our lives. How might each of us actually demonstrate practical love? What generous acts of giving might we make?

However, it can be harder to embrace the other part of Jesus' command: loving oneself. Christianity, as previous acknowledged, has an anxiety about 'self-love' as selfish and unattractive. However, if God loves each and every one of us, as we are and for who we are, who are we to put ourselves down?

So, this week, in addition to looking outwards, perhaps we should also look inwards ... not for the purposes of 'naval gazing', but to seek self-acceptance. One of the things I often say to those I offer spiritual direction to is remember that God not only loves you, but likes you. Liking oneself can be a lifetime's work, so perhaps now is a time to start. I remain convinced that practising the Examen, developed by St Ignatius, is a way of helping us do this. This is not an examen where we look at all our faults, but one in which we look, in prayer, to see where God has been active in our lives that day. This will produce, in my experience, one response: thankfulness. And that is a good place to start when it comes to liking oneself. To find out more about

the Examen you might wish to look at this website:
https://www.ignatianspirituality.com/ignatian-prayer/
the-examen/

Also, and don't underestimate this, please remember
that a little bit of pampering and enjoyment, even in
Lent, is not such a terrible thing. To allow oneself some
nice food, good company and a little bit of relaxation is
not wrong. As the great spiritual writer Gerry Hughes
was fond of saying, when we come before God for
judgment, he will ask us one question: 'Did you enjoy
my creation?' Let's dare to enjoy it, in the midst of the
struggle.

CLOSING PRAYER

God of All-Creation,
you make your world
in delight and for delight;
help us to know
we are your children
and enable us to walk in
the path of your love.
Call us home to ourselves
and enable us to respond,
through your Son, Jesus Christ. Amen.

WEEK 5

*'Still standing' – facing the truth
and starting again*

TO START YOU THINKING

As I write this book, the coronavirus pandemic continues to unfold around the world. Perhaps by the time you read it, it may have come to a more or less defined end; perhaps it will be called something else, or placed in the context of an even more frightening set of world of events. One thing I am already clear about is that the effects of the pandemic, at a personal, corporate, national and international level will be felt for a very long time. I am certainly not alone in recognising that for all of us this is a time of trauma. One doesn't need to have lost someone directly through COVID-19 or lost one's job or business to know this. Coronavirus represents one of those moments when the disruptions to our old ways of going on are experienced as so significant that we experience trauma. That trauma is certainly a trauma to the mind and to confidence and any number of things, but it is experienced through the body.

I suppose I am saying that we can all be the victims of circumstance. Clearly, one has to be careful here. The effects of something like coronavirus are clearly not experienced equally. Despite the rhetoric of 'we are all in this together', different people have experienced the crisis depending in large part on power and privilege, wealth, access to health care and colour of skin, alongside other factors. Nonetheless, at times of significant disruption or rupture, all of us have a story of trauma to tell. Just as with 9/11 or John F. Kennedy's assassination, there will be particular 'I was here' or 'this happened to me' stories to tell.

In recent years, I have become ever more alert to the shift in trauma language from 'victim', which has connotations of passivity and 'being done to', to the more active 'survivor'. I think this language is incredibly powerful. It has been significant in my own life as I've negotiated the ups and downs of living in a traumatised body. Through my body I've lived the realities of transphobia and disability, among other things. In time, I suspect the language of survival will become significant for many people negotiating the effects of twenty-first-century climate change, pandemics and inequity.

There is a clear sense in which Elton John may be read as a 'survivor', though I'm unsure whether he has ever described himself in those terms. This session examines what it might mean to say of him that he is 'still standing'. We shall look at how relationships help him not only to cope but to come to terms with a history of alcohol and drug abuse, empty sex, and exploitation by unscrupulous management. In one sense, this final session takes us back to the beginning of this 'journey': we explore how Elton's longing for love is found ultimately in a kind of reconciliation with his complex self and his unresolved past. He becomes a survivor by working and living through loss and trauma. This is not to be confused with embracing trauma as 'good' and 'necessary', but discovering that trauma does not define, control and limit. It is survived, even as the past continues to exist as a trace in his life.

I appreciate that some people might struggle to place this language of 'survival' in the wider Christian story. It might strike some as too much 'self-help' and too little 'gospel'. I hear this. However, it is important to recognise that there has been some significant theology about both trauma and the notion of survival. Here, I invite you to consider one example: the theology of Dolores Williams.

Dolores Williams' work is part of what has come to be known as 'womanist theology'. This is theology written by African-American women using a liberationist perspective. It is typically critical of 'feminist theology', whilst being seen as allied to it. It emerged out of African-American and global majority women's recognition that feminists often don't speak for or include them. Too often 'feminism' speaks from a middle-class white perspective. As a white middle-class feminist, I am keen to avoid appropriating Williams' insights. Rather I present a key moment which clarifies why survival can be an important theological category.

In *Sisters in the Wilderness,* Williams analyses the story of Hagar, found in Genesis 16, through a womanist lens. It's worth saying that Hagar's story has been represented in theological discourse as an example of what Phyllis Trible calls 'a text of terror' – that is, a text used to frighten, regulate and demean women; however, Williams, among others, has sought to recover Hagar for a liberative reading of religion.

Hagar is the slave girl whom Sarai/Sarah instructs Abram/Abraham to have sex with in order for them to have a child. Williams does not shy away from Hagar's status as a victim of Sarah and Abraham's violence and exploitation. However, she also draws attention to often ignored features about the Hagar myth: firstly, Hagar has the courage to choose her own way, even though that way means likely death in the desert. Though she initially cannot avoid being used by Abraham, she runs away into the wilderness, determined to follow her own path. Secondly, while in the wilderness Hagar receives a blessing from God. Not only does she come upon an oasis of water, she is told she will bear a son Ishmael and, through this son, she will be the mother of an entire nation.

Significantly, God speaks directly to Hagar. This is the first time in the Bible that any woman is spoken to by God without the presence of a male figure. Even Eve does not get a 'one-to-one' with God. Sarah – patriarchy's chosen vessel and lawful wife of Abraham – only overhears God's promise that she will, at a great age, bear a son. In the stories of the patriarchs – of Abraham, Moses and so on – only men get to speak directly with God.

Perhaps, even more powerfully, Hagar does something truly remarkable: she names God. Genesis 16:13-14 runs: 'So she named the Lord who spoke to her, "You are El-roi" (the God who sees); for she said, "Have I really seen God and remained alive after seeing him?" Therefore, the well was called Beer-lahai-roi; it lies between Kadesh and Bered.' Not only does she claim the male authority of naming – by naming a well – but she does something not even the greatest Patriarch is allowed to do.

Hagar, the black slave, runs off and receives a blessing from God. She then names God. She performs Adam's role as the maker of names and names God. Certainly, while she is told by God to return to Abraham's household and slavery, Hagar does so renewed. She returns not a frightened slave, but a promise bearer – she's chosen by God as the mother of a great nation. She returns because the survival of her child, of her promise, depends on the practical sustenance Abraham's household offers; however, when she returns she has filled with a new power. She carries, then, subversion in her being. Her fecundity is no longer passive but active; her fecundity subverts the established narrative and plot.

This is a picture of resurrection which should make us sit up and take note. As already indicated, I don't want to appropriate Williams' analysis of Hagar. Rather, I want to draw our attention to the power of a story where a person who is lost in the wilderness claims power and, more than that, survives with the assurance of God's promises. This survival, for Williams, is resurrection because, for many of us in a damaged world, 'survival' is enough and more than enough. This is not survival at the basest, meanest level, but survival which changes the world. Hagar returns to a horrible situation because she needs to do that for Ishmael to survive. But she returns no longer powerless. Through God, she transforms fate into destiny.

As we meditate on Elton's attempts to come to terms with himself and others in this final session of *Still Standing,* I do not want to suggest that he is a Hagar figure. Far from it. Rather, I want to invite us to be alert to the way in which the denouement of *Rocketman* can be read through a lens which sees 'resurrection' as 'survival'. Whatever we may think of Elton as a person, in embracing 'rehab' and the way of 'self-acceptance' he commits himself to survival. Not mere survival, but a way of hope and rejoicing, and a life built on promises. That is surely a life worth celebrating. That is a life which dares to draw closer to the invitations of the Living God.

PRAYER

Living God,
we give you thanks
that in your solidarity with us
you are prepared to travel
the path of suffering and death
and show forth the way of true life.
Grant us the courage
to stand with you in your hour of need;
to resist hate and violence,
and be your people of justice and truth.
Amen.

Icebreaker
If someone were to ask you to give an example of
resurrection or survival or new life in your experience,
what might you share? To what extent, if any, do you
connect that story of survival with faith in Jesus Christ?

WATCH

Chapter 17 (1.34.05 to 1.41.35): The end of the (yellow brick) road

Elton is lost in self-pity and self-destruction and has a disastrous dinner with his best and oldest friend Bernie. Elton expresses his sense of disappointment with Bernie, claiming that Bernie has repeatedly abandoned him. Bernie counters by asking when Elton gave up. He tells Elton that it is not weak to ask for help. When Elton says some cruel things in response, Bernie leaves, singing a version of 'Goodbye Yellow Brick Road'.[7] Elton feels completely abandoned and returns home. He realises he has probably lost his last friend and collapses into a drug-induced paranoia. He overdoses. Meanwhile Reid assures the promoter of Elton's tour that, as usual, he will get Elton fit to perform. The promoter is horrified, but does not pull the gigs. As Elton gets ready to perform he finally realises he needs help and goes into rehab. He abandons the 'magic land of Oz', says goodbye to the 'yellow brick road', and faces reality at last.

What strikes you about this scene? What do you make, for example, of Bernie's response to Elton's inability to face facts? Is it reasonable? What do you make of Elton?

---

[7] You can find the lyrics here: https://genius.com/Elton-john-goodbye-yel-low-brick-road-lyrics

Have you ever been in situations or friendships where you or another person has been unable to face the reality of the situation? (Please only share what you feel safe to share.) How has that felt? What did you need to do in order to face up to them?

'Oz' and the 'Yellow Brick Road' are powerful symbols of escapism, our need for fantasies, and of dreams and magic. Does 'growing up' and self-acceptance mean we have to give up on these fantastical and imaginary spaces? What, if anything, can be helpful about keeping a place for 'magic' in our lives?

What in the end leads Elton to seek rehab? How do you feel when Elton finally abandons Reid and the shows? (How would you feel if you'd been in the audience of one of the abandoned shows?)

GOING DEEPER

Read
Acts 8:1-3, 9:1-21: The Conversion of Saul

It might surprise some users of *Still Standing* that I juxtapose Elton's moment of decision with the biblical story of Saul. I understand this. There are many differences between the story of Saul, the persecutor who becomes St Paul, and Elton John, the world-famous rock star. Nonetheless, the story of Saul stands as one of the great conversion moments in world history. The notion of a 'Damascene conversion' has achieved escape velocity from the religious context which generated it. I will leave it up to you to decide whether Elton has a 'Damascene conversion' or not. However, just as Saul/Paul comes to recognise that his whole approach to the world has to be re-formed and changed, surely the same applies to Elton.

In what ways might we read Elton's 'turn towards

the light' as akin to Saul/Paul's? In what ways are these stories very different?

Have you ever had a redemption moment? The word 'repent' means, in Greek, 'turn around'. Even if you haven't experienced a full conversion experience, have you experienced the phenomenon of 'turning around' to face the truth? If so, what enabled you to do that? How has your life changed?

Who or what, in your view, needs to undergo a 'Damascene conversion' in our present age? Who in your view are the people who persecute the 'people of God' (interpret that as widely or narrowly as you like!)?

What would you say to someone who said that individual 'conversions', such as those experienced by Elton or Saul, are all very well, but the real 'Damascene conversions' must be cultural, i.e. that as a society we need to have our 'inner eyes' opened to the stains of racism or transphobia or how we are destroying the planet.

WATCH

From 1.41.35 to 1.45.07 – Time to face the truth …

(Note: This clip uses a word which many find taboo and deeply offensive.)

In group therapy, Elton finally takes responsibility for his actions. He realises he's hated himself for years and he needs to begin again. He realises he's resented things that don't matter – the lack of his birth father's affection or his mother's approval. He wonders if he should have tried to be more ordinary. As he explores his past, figures from his life appear, including his Nan, one of the people who always believed in his talent. He makes peace with his mum, who he feels has always resented him. He asks for forgiveness, and says they need to forgive each other. Reid appears and claims that Elton's selfishness is what prevents him from self-acceptance. Elton says that his problem was that he believed that Reid – a man who cannot love – loved Elton back. Finally, Elton accepts his difference and strangeness, letting go of his conventional birth-father's approval. Bernie tells Elton that he simply needs to remember who he is and be okay with it. When Reid claims Elton doesn't know who he is, Elton says he does: he is 'Elton Hercules John.' This leaves only Elton the small child – little Reggie – to ask, 'When are you going to hug me?' It is the final reconciliation with his past. A hug of self-acceptance.

What is your initial reaction to this scene? Why?

What do you make of Elton's acceptance of his 'strangeness'. Is this something we are all called to do? Or do you feel you are not strange at all? What would you say to someone who says that 'strangeness' is a marker of God (given that God's love is so intense and profound, and therefore so strange, that we can barely cope with it)?

What do you make of the interaction between the grown-up Elton and the young Reggie? When Elton claims he is 'Elton Hercules John' has he erased Reggie?

How do you react when young Reggie asks of Elton, 'When are you going to hug me?' Why do you think you react that way?

Have you ever had to reconcile with your past? What was that experience like? What have you learned? What did it enable you to offer to others?

GOING DEEPER

Read
John 21:9-19 – On the Seashore…

Of all the resurrection encounters, this is arguably the most beautiful and among the most touching. Here Peter, back at work as a fisherman, encounters Jesus on the shore. He rejoices to see his Lord! They share food and Jesus asks Peter if he loves him. He asks Peter this question three times, and Peter reassures him each time. This is an echo, of course, of the three times Peter denies Jesus on the night of his arrest. Jesus instructs Peter to 'feed his sheep' and also says that when Peter is old he will be bound to a cross and be crucified like his Lord. Jesus instructs Peter to follow him.

What is your initial response to this passage? Do you like it? What puzzles you or invites you in?

Does it stand as a powerful story about becoming or being a mature follower of Jesus? That is, when we are young or young-in-faith, often we get distracted and lost and deny the truth of God; however, as mature Christians we are invited to stand up for what really matters, even if that leads to death. Or is it more complicated than that?

To what extent has Elton travelled on a similar trajectory to Peter? In Peter's youth he is passionate and determined to be active and be the first ... but in maturity he will take on new responsibility and learn that being a leader requires sacrifice rather than self-indulgence ...

What are the truths and responsibilities we need to face in our lives? How do you think Jesus sees you? Do you feel as beloved as Peter?

WATCH

1.45.08 – 1.50.43: Still Standing …

As Elton cleans the floor in the rehab centre, Bernie comes to visit. They chat warmly and honestly, and Elton is scared he won't be any good at writing music now that he is clean of drugs and alcohol. Bernie astutely points out that Elton is scared to feel. As a gift, Bernie offers him the lyrics for a new song and encourages Elton to set them. As Bernie leaves and Elton thanks him for all his support, Bernie says, 'You're my brother.' Elton tentatively enters the music therapy room and slowly allows himself to 'feel again'. 'Still Standing' comes together. As the movie closes, we see Elton performing in the video which accompanied the 1987 single release. Finally, Elton is congruent: he embraces his identity as a showman, and finds himself at ease with who he is as a gay man. As the credits roll we see how Elton's life has come together since getting clean: a happy marriage to David Furnish, raising his kids, setting up an important international AIDS charity work and managing his ongoing love of shopping!

To what extent does Bernie put his finger on the real issue: Elton is afraid to feel? Have you ever been in situations where you've been afraid to feel? What was that like?

What do we learn about Elton and Bernie's friendship in this scene?

Given that music has always been Elton's outlet, is it understandable that he is afraid to feel?

How do you feel as the film ends? Are you pleased? Disappointed? Satisfied?

How satisfying do you find the idea of 'still standing' as a metaphor for resurrection? What other images might you be inclined to use?

GOING DEEPER

Read
John 20:1-18 – An Encounter in the Garden of Resurrection

Perhaps I am just a sucker for resurrection stories, but I adore the scene unfolded in this part of John's gospel. It has it all: the boldness of a woman prepared to seek out the one she loves, the surprise of an empty tomb, and men struggling to catch up with what a woman already knows. It also has a moment of mysterious encounter, when the still-shocked Mary Magdalene meets Jesus as she has never seen him before. It is a moment of recognition. As she hears her name, Mary recognises the Risen Lord. In a few short verses, we encounter grief, hope, shock and the blessing of new life. In those verses, Mary's life is transformed and we rejoice with her.

How do you respond to hearing this passage of scripture again (or for the first time)? What strikes you or stands out for you?

What would you say to the suggestion that, in an intense miniature, Mary goes through the emotional journey that Elton goes through in rehab? Have you ever undertaken a process (perhaps in coming to terms with loss), that has taken you on a process of 're-reading' reality? How akin is that experience to the one Mary encounters in the Garden?

In the final scene of *Rocketman*, Bernie gives Elton the gift of a new song … what gift/s does Jesus offer to Mary (and us)?

It is when Mary hears her name spoken by Jesus that she recognises him. How important is it for us to feel called by name?

How can we take the stories of Elton's 'resurrection' and Jesus' definitive resurrection forward into our lives as the course ends?

LOOKING AHEAD ... ACTIVITIES TO CONSIDER THIS WEEK

The world in which we live can feel a difficult and unpleasant place. Certainly, in an age of vulgar populism and nativism, those whose faces don't fit or lives are seen as second-best, feel the sharpest cut of injustice and inequality. Yet, for all that, the world does remain a site of promise and hope. God is active and alive and we are called to play our part in being God's body.

There are many ways we can add our voices and lives to the work of love and justice that is already being undertaken. This week, investigate local, regional and international charities which work to foreground marginalised lives and see how you and your community can support. One doesn't need to have the resources of an Elton John to make a difference.

Equally, it may be that in the light of this week's session you and your community might want to explore how you can work to support those in need of opportunities to turn their lives around. Charities and Networks from Alcoholics Anonymous through to Mind and Turning Point are under great pressure during this time of great economic pain. See how you might be a person or community that makes a difference to those living with addiction and all the side-effects it generates.

CLOSING PRAYER

Risen Lord,
in your Resurrection,
you lift up your pilgrim people;
may we embrace your victory,
not so we can lord it over others
but discover that in service,
and service towards the least of all,
we may take our place with you
at your open table. Amen.

POSTSCRIPT

I hope you have both enjoyed and been stimulated by this course. Most of all, I hope it's helped you be ever more alert to how God and God's work can be discerned in film and culture. If you've stayed with *Still Standing* this far, I trust that – even if you were initially suspicious – you've discovered that even a life as riotous and naughty as that led by the younger Elton John can reveal the promise and possibilities of the Living God.

Where to now? I guess that is up to you. A couple of suggestions. Firstly, one of the many wonderful things about Darton, Longman and Todd as a publisher is their fearless determination to produce Christian study guides that take people out beyond the obvious. Do check out their website and back catalogue. If you've enjoyed this course, I guarantee you will find others they've published that can be used not only during Lent but throughout the year.

Secondly, I hope this book inspires you to engage with cinema and other forms of visual culture with fresh eyes. While I would be cautious about saying that every film or TV show is 'about God', God is there waiting to be found in the most surprising places. Dare to take a look. God is so vibrantly alive in this world, it is practically impossible to keep her out of things. So, from time to time, take a risk and dare to watch films with a fresh eye. God, in my experience, has usually got there before us.